Poems For Funerals
&
Those Who Grieve

Other books of Angel-Inspired Poetry
by Faye Kilday

Angels Speaking
Love Poems For Love's Sake

Poems For Funerals
&
Those Who Grieve

Angel-Inspired Poetry By
Faye Kilday

Angel-Inspired Poetry

Angel-Inspired Poetry

"Poetry Made For Sharing!"

Website and Email Address

www.angel-inspiredpoetry.com

angelinspiredpoetry@yahoo.co.nz

First published in 2003 by Angel-Inspired Poetry

This edition published in 2006 by Angel-Inspired Poetry
in association with Lulu Press, Inc

ISBN 978-1-84728-455-6

Using the poems in this book

Your Soul Remembers

When you read words of wisdom and truth...
Inspiring words that touch your heart,
It's simply the work of a messenger playing
their heavenly part
In helping your soul remember something
it already knows...
And at this time of remembering your soul
blossoms and grows!

Contents

Sorrow

To my own special angels in Heaven...

my father William
(1940 - 1979)
and
my grandmother Hilda
(1914 - 1981)

A gentle breath upon my cheek
when there's no one there,
Objects that go missing and
then mysteriously reappear;
Inspiring images in my mind
or a helpful or clever idea
Constantly remind me that my
family in spirit are near.

Introduction

In February, 2003, I was in my local library, quietly browsing through the poetry books, when I was joined by an angel in disguise! She appeared by my side with a librarian, asked the librarian if there were any books containing poems for funerals to which the librarian replied, "I'm not sure... I think so..." and then they both wandered off towards a computer.

Now, you may be thinking that this all seems very ordinary and how could I possibly think that this normal-looking lady was an angel in disguise? That is until you realize that I write Angel-Inspired Poetry. And the last few months before this encounter occurred I had been feeling anxious and lost. I had a feeling I was suppose to be doing "something" but I didn't know what.

And the angels hadn't been speaking to me. Or rather, they *had* been speaking to me, but I had been too self-absorbed to hear them. So they sent in one of their own and practically yelled in my ear. And this time I heard them; loud and clear! Yes, that normal-looking lady was an angel in disguise!

I left the library that day on cloud nine - I felt like I had my own pair of angelic wings. And I knew that the "something" I was supposed to be doing was writing and publishing a book of poems for funerals.

To satisfy my curiosity I went back to the library the following day to see if there *were* any books of poems for funerals. I found a couple, mostly containing poems that were written a long time ago, and I was quite surprised to see that they were still on the shelf (perhaps angels don't have library cards).

Anyway, I mentioned that the books contained poems that were written a long time ago because, whilst many of these poems were written by famous poets who I personally admire, I know it's true that many people can't relate to the language or style that these poems are written in.

The angels speak to me in a simple language - probably because I'm a simple person (no, that's not an insult. Simplicity is the key to a happy life!) And as I act as a channel by writing words as I see, or sometimes hear them in my mind, my poems are simple and easy to understand.

And so, *Poems For Funerals* was conceived (*& Those Who Grieve* was added later when I realized many of the poems will be of comfort to people who are grieving). An unexpected but very pleasant surprise. And 5 days before my birthday too - the best gift I received and I bet my father, who's one of my angels, arranged it!

I hope these poems speak to you in the same warm and encouraging way they spoke to me as I was writing them. And if any of them do speak to you then remember - they were angel-inspired. I was simply the messenger!

Faye Kilday

Eternity

'Everyone who dies will live again'

Metamorphosis

Beneath the light of a radiant moon,
The caterpillar's spinning a silk cocoon.
Wrapping itself in threads of gold,
A truly magical sight to behold.
And when it's finished it will rest
in its shell,
And then, just like a magic spell,
The caterpillar's cocoon will die...
To reveal a beautiful butterfly!

Heaven's Beauty

The world is a marvellous
and mysterious place,
Shaped by God's hand and
blessed with His grace.
But no place on Earth,
however grand it may be,
Could ever compare with
Heaven's beauty!

Our Special Place In Heaven

There's a special place in Heaven
that's reserved for you and I,
A special little place in our
home up in the sky.
And if God calls me to Heaven
and I reach it before you,
I promise I'll take care of it
the way you'd want me to.
I will keep it warm and tidy -
the way you like a home to be,
And I'll brighten it with Heaven's
flowers, angels' songs and poetry.

A Dream Called Death

"Death" is such a final word -
it fills your heart with pain,
It makes you think you'll never see
your loved ones again;
It makes you think you'll never rest
your eyes upon their face,
It makes you think you'll never feel
their touch or warm embrace...
But personally I think it's all a sad
and sorry lie that some poor soul
invented because *they* were afraid
to die!
Think about it for a while and I'm
sure you'll see my point of view...
Because inside and outside every one
of you is spirit - the spirit of every
living thing both above and beneath
the skies,
Hidden from view of most of you by
your mortal human eyes.
But it's there alright - spirit is real...
You're aware of its presence when
you think and feel,
You're aware of its presence when
you meditate and pray...

You're aware of spirit's presence
every day in every way.
And as spirit is a part of God it makes
no sense to me,
Why some people find it impossible
to believe in eternity!
Your body ceases to operate - the
blood flows from your heart,
But your spirit - your thinking,
feeling part - simply leaves your
body and with divine intention
Goes to another plane - to a spiritual
dimension.
For the death state is a spiritual
journey - it's not as scary as it seems,
And each of you experience the death
state each night in your dreams!
So imagine your most vivid dream -
a dream where you felt at peace,
A dream where beauty filled your heart
and you felt your worries cease,
And then you'll get a feeling for what
it's like to die,
To explore new worlds and dimensions -
to spread your wings and fly!

So *live your life* unafraid of what
death holds in store...

For when your earthly time is through
there'll be new worlds to explore.
And live your life enlightened to the
fact that all around you,
Your loved ones in the spirit world
protect you and surround you!

When a Child Dies

When a child dies we ask
ourselves, "Why?"
Why did God take one
so young...
One whose life was fun
and carefree,
One whose life had just begun.

When a child dies we feel
heartbroken and sad,
But the angels in Heaven
rejoice and are glad,
For as we're sadly
wondering, "Why?"
An angel is being welcomed
to its home in the sky.

To its new home in Heaven,
its new home in bliss,
This angel is welcomed
with a heavenly kiss.
And the air is filled with
song as each angel sings
Of life here in Heaven
and the joy that it brings.

When a child dies we ask
ourselves, "Why?"
Why did God take one
so young...
One whose life is fun
and carefree,
One whose life has just begun...

Everyone Lives Again

Everyone who smiles
will someday cry,
Everyone who lives
will someday die.
But everyone who cries
will be freed from pain,
And everyone who dies
will live again.

Beyond The Skies

This very clever human race
Can see as far as outer space;
But with our mortal human eyes,
When we look up into the skies,
We cannot see the streets of gold
Whose paths are walked by
young and old.

But just because we cannot trace
The exact spot of this heavenly place
Doesn't mean that it's not there,
It only means that way down here
Us humans need to realize
Someday we'll go beyond the skies
To this beautiful, heavenly place above,
Where we'll live eternally in love.

Goodbye Is Not Forever

Goodbye is not forever dear,
so don't be filled with pain,
For when the time is right
we will both meet up again.
When God calls you to Heaven
we will meet up face to face,
And you'll hear my gentle welcome
and you'll feel my warm embrace.
So don't be sad my darling for
we'll meet again you'll see,
And we'll spend our time together
in eternal ecstasy!

Where Is Heaven?

Where is Heaven?
Is it somewhere in outer space?
Where does my loved one now dwell...
In some far and distant place?

Heaven is all around you...
It's as close as the air and love
that surround you.
Heaven is everywhere - it's not
just in the skies,
It's a spiritual dimension that can't
be seen through human eyes.

How do I know my loved one is safe?
How do I know they are well?
How do I know that they made it to Heaven?
Is there any way I can tell?

Your loved one is well in Heaven
because they're surrounded by
God's love and care,
And I can promise you that they
made it to Heaven, because an
angel guided them there!

Is there any way I can tell them how
much they meant (and still mean) to me?
I'm not sure how to contact them, do you
know what Heaven's address could be?

Just talk... and know that they
hear you,
Because you'll never be truly apart;
And Heaven's address?
Well now, that's simple...
Just send your thoughts care of
your heart!

Inspiration

*'Eventually the clouds will part and
let the sun shine through'*

God's Is The Greatest Power

Some people don't believe in God,
they say that He is fake,
To them I say, "Just look around,
for no one else could make such
perfect, natural beauty - like that
found in a flower."
Us humans may be clever but
God's is the greatest power!

Animals Go To Heaven Too

Animals go to Heaven too
When their time on Earth is through;
And those who were pets lovingly wait
To greet their owners at Heaven's gate.

Above Grey Clouds

Whenever I am feeling sad this is
what I do...
I remind myself that above grey
clouds is a beautiful sky of blue;
And eventually the clouds will
part and let the sun shine through.

Sisters Are Special People

Sisters are guardian angels
that lend a helping hand,
Sisters are special friends
who care and understand,
Sisters are rays of sunshine
that brighten the darkest day,
Sisters are special people in
every kind of way!

Mothers Are a Special Gift

Mothers are a special gift sent
from God above,
They bless us with their nurturing,
And fill us with their love.

They pick us up when we are down,
And when we're sad they know,
They're always there to lend a hand,
And guide us as we go.

And mothers are like special jewels
that can't be bought or sold -
A mother's love's more precious
than the rarest gem or gold.

Yes, mothers are a special gift sent
from God above,
And we'll be blessed forever with
their never-ending love!

A Blessing In Disguise

When I was six years old
my father passed away,
I can still remember how
I felt on that cold, sad,
winter's day;
I can still feel that sense
of numbness as my heart
filled up with pain,
And I guess, if the truth be
known, I thought I'd never
see him again.

Well the years have flown
by since then and with time
I've grown wise,
And I now feel that my
father's death was a
blessing in disguise.
Of course I wish he was
still alive and of course
I still feel pain,
But I know now that he
guides me and I know we'll
meet again.

But my father's death was
a miracle and a blessing
in disguise,
Because it helped me look
within myself and it opened
up my eyes.
And through my deep soul
searching I got answers
from above -
Answers that made me cry
with gratitude and filled my
heart with love.

I've shared many of these
answers and messages
I've received,
And I feel truly blessed that
they've helped many people -
especially those who grieved.

So once again I want to take
your hand within my hand,
And share with you a message
that might help you understand
The reason why some people
die when they've only just
been born,
And the reason others live
to see the glorious golden dawn.

The length of time we stay alive -
how long we choose to live,
Depends upon what we have
to receive and on what we
have to give.

For some the experience of
birth upon the Earth below,
Is all their soul requires to
become enlightened and
to grow.
Whilst others' souls may be
at an entirely different stage,
And they may require the
experience of living to old age.

The thing to remember is that
the Earth is a school - a wonderful
gift to the soul,
And everything that happens is
within God's divine control.

When my father died I felt
abandoned and left alone,
But now I know that his death
means I am never on my own;
Because I know he walks beside me,
he's only a thought away,

And I know he works with the
angels to guide me every day.
And through his life he made the
world a nicer place to be,
And he passed his precious gift
of creativity on to me.

So whether a person lives for a
short while - or until they're
old and wise,
Remember, each soul's purpose
has meaning and is a blessing
in disguise.

And you'll find this easier to
remember - it'll be easier to see,
If you ask yourself, "What gifts
has this soul given to the world?"
And...
"What gifts have they given to me?"

The Human Race Can Learn a Lot From Space

When you go outside on a clear night
and look up at the magical scene above,
If you're anything like me you feel
inspired by gratitude and love.

And as you watch in wonder the stars,
sparkling like diamonds in the sky, it
brings a tear to your eye;
And you realize just how magnificent
our Creator is to have created all this.

And it makes you think that if you
could view your life from a star
You'd realize just how insignificant
your worries really are!

I Believe

I believe in angels and
I believe in God above,
I believe in miracles and
I believe in love.
I believe in Heaven and
I believe that when I die
I will walk down streets of gold
in my new home in the sky.

I believe in having fun and
I believe that dreams come true,
I believe in beauty and
I believe in magic too.
I believe that faith can heal
and that broken hearts will mend,
I believe in friendship and
I believe in you, my friend!

Healing

*'Only time can heal a heart
that's broken and torn all apart'*

The Best Cures

The best cures, to heal a variety
of ills, are free...
The best medicine is laughter,
The best comforter is a hug,
The best soul-reviver is a smile,
And love is by far the best drug!

Time

Only time can heal a heart
that's broken and torn all apart;
And time alone will heal the pain,
And reunite loved ones again.

Whenever You Are Feeling Sad

Whenever you are feeling sad,
whenever you are blue,
Hold this poem to your heart
and know I think of you.
Then imagine golden healing-light
cascading from above,
And feel your sadness leaving
as your soul is filled with love.

Thank You

'Thank you for simply being there'

It's Never Too Late To Say Thank You

You touched my life in so
many wonderful ways;
And I'm not sure if I remembered
to say thank you.

You inspired me with your
encouragement and words
of praise;
And I'm not sure if I remembered
to say thank you.

When I needed a hand you always
had one to lend,
You were, in every way, a true friend;
And I'm not sure if I remembered
to say thank you.

And now I can't say it to your face.
But still, I feel you near.

So here's two important words that
I *want* to say and you *need* to hear...

THANK YOU!

Thank You

Thank you for relieving a little
of my strain,
Thank you for absorbing
a little of my pain.

Thank you for taking control when
I was paralysed by shock,
Thank you for staying grounded
and solid as a rock.

Thank you for crying with me and
when I cried alone
Thank you for not leaving me all
on my own.

Thank you for your kindness,
your comfort and your care,
But most of all thank you for
simply being there.

A Word Of Thanks

When I was in need of help you kindly
lent a hand,
For this I'm very grateful and want you
to understand
That your kindness really touched me -
You're an angel through and through,
And I hope and pray that someday
I can do the same for you!

Angels

'An angel will guide us to Heaven's door'

Angels In Disguise

Who was that kind stranger who
helped you cross the road?
And who was that Samaritan who
helped you with your load?
And that stranger at the bus stop
who talked with you awhile,
And turned the frown upon your
face into a happy smile?

Why, angels in disguise, of course!
That's who these souls must be,
Sent by God in Heaven to help folks
like you and me!

Their gentle ways and kind displays -
the little things they do,
Help us when we need a hand -
or feel a little blue!

So the next time you are helped by
someone you don't recognize,
It's possible that they may be
an angel in disguise!

No One Dies Alone

The other day I went to the cemetery
to remember loved ones dear to me,
When I noticed a woman gently shaking,
and I knew at a glance that her heart was
aching.
I was going to walk on, I didn't want to
intrude, but I felt in my heart this was
thoughtless and rude;
So I asked God to guide me, so I'd know
what to say, then I took a deep breath and
walked over her way.
She was sitting in silence, by a grave side,
And her eyes were still red from the tears
she had cried.
I stood still beside her and said, with a smile,
"I was wondering if you'd like to talk for
a while?"
She didn't reply and I was ready to leave,
when she said, in a whisper, "It's so hard
to believe - a year ago today my son
was stolen away - he was taken from me
in the blink of an eye; it seems so unfair
that he had to die!
But the thing I can't accept is... he was
on his own; why oh why did God let
him die alone?"

51

I sat down beside her and looked into her
eyes,
Then I told her, "No man is alone when
he dies!
When the angel of death knocked upon your
son's door; when his earthly body wasn't
needed anymore;
God sent an angel to take your son's hand
and accompany him to the promised land!"

With hope in her eyes she asked,"Do you
believe that is true?"
I assured her with a smile and replied, "Yes,
I do."

"For although we can't see them with our
mortal eyes, when every one of us eventually
dies... there'll be an angel with an outstretched
hand to guide us to the promised land.
For life is such a fragile thing and none of us
know what each day will bring;
But there's one thing of which we can all be
sure - an angel will guide us to Heaven's
door!"

I hoped that my message would help ease her
grief; that what I had said would bring some
relief.

And I knew God had helped me to know
what to say, so I decided to leave her and get
on with my day.
I didn't wait for her to reply, but I silently
blest her and said goodbye.
And as I turned to walk away, she touched
my hand and I heard her say, "The past year
has been hell, filled with heartache and strife -
so I thank God for sending you into my life.
I'm eternally grateful for the kindness you've
shown, and for helping me realize my son
did not die alone!"

At Sometime, You'll Hear Them Speaking

Sometimes, when I feel alone,
When there's no one else at home but me,
And there's nothing worth watching
on the TV,
And all my friends have gone away
On some exotic holiday,
I can get a little sad, and have thoughts
which leave me feeling bad.

And then I hear them speaking...

And I thank God that the angels are
by my side.
I thank God that the angels don't try
to hide their love for me.
And I thank God that we'll love each
other for all eternity.

At sometime, when you're all alone,
When there's no one else at home but you,
And you're feeling a little unsure about
what to do;
When your friends have gone on holiday
or simply choose to stay away,

You might feel a little sad,
And have thoughts which leave you
feeling bad,
And then you might read something
inspiring that touches your heart,
Or have an uplifting thought or feeling
which hits you like a dart.

And as you hear them speaking...

You'll thank God that the angels are
by your side.
You'll thank God that the angels don't
try to hide their love for you.
And you'll thank God that you'll love
each other until, and after, your time
on Earth is through.

Heavenly Dream Team

I don't care,
I have no fear,
Because I know that you
are always near.

You're always there
when I feel alone,
You're always around when
there's no one at home.

You never leave me,
You're only a thought away,
You're by my side every
single night and day.

And if I walked through
the fires of hell,
You'd hold my hand;
And if I was feeling anxious,
You'd understand.

You're my guardian angel,
You wrap me in your
wings of love;
You're my spiritual best friend,
A special gift from God above.

And when my time on Earth
is through, you'll take
my hand,
I know I can depend on you to
take me to the promised land.

Because we're a heavenly
dream team
And there's nothing that
we can't do,
So hold me close sweet angel,
And know that I love you
too...

Our love will always see us through!

The Feather

This isn't a poem but it's based on a vision I had and I thought you might enjoy reading it.

"I'm going to sleep," I told you. "But in case you slip away whilst I'm sleeping, I want you to know that I love you!" And as I slept I dreamt that the most beautiful angel lifted your spirit from your body and guided you to a tunnel of golden light that radiated from the ceiling. But before you entered the golden tunnel you turned to the angel and said, "Wait, there's something I have to do." Then you drifted back to the bed where I slept, my head resting peacefully on your arm, and you gently brushed aside my hair and kissed my cheek. "I love you too," you said, "See you soon..." and then you went back to the tunnel and with an ecstatic heart, entered it, the angel close behind. And then there was just the plain, white ceiling. And when I awoke the next morning you were dead and a white feather lay next to your pillow - which is very peculiar because your pillow is made of sponge, not feathers...

Continuing Presence

*'A truly successful life is one whose value
remains when its work is done'*

Looking For Grandma

Grandma said, before she died,
That if I look up at the sky
at night,
And look for the biggest and
brightest star,
That will be her watching me
from afar.

Tall Poppy

Be great. Shine bright.
Light up the world at night.
Go far. Fly high.
Carve your name into the sky.
Be bold. Be YOU.
Show everyone what YOU can do.
Be inspiring. Be courageous.
Let your success become contagious.
Be immortal. Create history...
Be the best that you can be!

Butterfly Kisses

The strangest thing happened to me today...
I was sitting in the garden, pleasantly
passing the time away, when I started
thinking of you.

I remembered how much you loved the
outdoors and being amongst the flowers;
I remembered you sitting under the apple
tree, passing away the hours.

When suddenly I noticed movement out
of the corner of my eye,
So I turned to see what it was - and saw
a butterfly.

A beautiful butterfly with white and gold
wings - like nothing I'd seen before,
Resting on the rosebush - the one you
used to adore.

It stayed there for a while and then, most
graciously, it spread its lovely wings
and headed towards me.

It fluttered around my head and then,
too stunned to speak, I watched it flutter
to my face and gently touch my cheek.

It touched my other cheek and then I
watched it go away;
It fluttered off into the blue skies of
the summer day.

And as I sat and wondered, without
an explanation,
I realized what had happened and
my heart filled with elation.

For I now know that today I fulfilled
one of my wishes...
I felt your loving touch again in the
form of butterfly kisses.

A Truly Successful Life

A truly successful life is one
that's filled with laughter,
love and fun.
That laughs in the faces of
failure and fear,
That is always helpful and
happy to share.
That knows what it's like
to never give in,
That knows what it's like
to succeed and win.
That follows its heart and
is always sincere,
That enriches the lives of
all who draw near...
A truly successful life is one
whose value remains when
its work is done.

True Friendship Lasts Forever

True friendship lasts forever like a
powerful binding glue,
For true friends are bound together
by a love that's strong and true.

And although time may divide them
and they may be miles apart,
True friends will stay together in
the boundaries of the heart.

And when they're reunited,
as eventually they'll be,
They'll walk hand in hand together
down the lanes of memory...

Remembering the good times,
reflecting on the sad;
Remembering the love they shared
and all the fun they had.

And they'll look towards the future
with happiness and cheer,
For true friendship grows more stronger
with the passing of each year.

The Brightest Star

When the angel of death has come
for me I'll not have gone too far,
Look to the sky and you will see a
bright and shining star...
That will be my sign to let you
know all's well
In paradise, where I have gone,
and evermore will dwell!

Together

We will never be apart
Whilst you dwell in my heart.

The Visitor

I visited you today.
I spoke to you, but you didn't
hear what I had to say,
or feel me wipe your tears away...

Hope

'Never lose hope for a better tomorrow'

There Is More Than Meets The Eye

The world is a wonderful and
mysterious place,
There is so much more than
the human race
And the animals and plants
that inhabit the land -
There are mysteries and marvels
we don't understand.

For God has blessed us with
mortal eyes,
So we don't learn the mysteries
and become too wise.
But instead we must believe
with faith and love
That there is a Heaven
up above;
That angels guide us every day -
helping us along life's way...

That each day holds a new
surprise - or maybe a miracle
in disguise.
For the mysteries and marvels
that we can't retrace
Prove that the world's an
incredible place!

Never Lose Hope

When you're faced with sadness,
heartache and sorrow
Never lose hope for a better
tomorrow,
For a large dose of hope is
just what you need
When you feel you are failing
but long to succeed.

For hope brings expectance -
that your dreams will come true,
And hope gives you something
to look forward to.
So never lose hope for tomorrow
you'll see,
Will be better and brighter than
you dreamed it could be!

Some Things Never Change

Loving hearts will always be remembered,
Shining lights will never fade away;
Gentle souls will remain that way forever...
And happy memories are here to stay.

A Symbol Of Hope

The rosebud quietly grows in spring,
Quite unaware of the joy it will bring;
Never knowing that soon it will help
someone cope -
As a symbol from God it portrays
love and hope.

By Any Other Name

Life, by any other name, would still
be a miracle.
Our world, by any other name, would
still be as beautiful.
Love, by any other name, would still
be pure energy.
Creation, by any other name, would
still be a mystery.
Miracles, by any other name, would
still be as nice.
And Heaven, by any other name,
would still be paradise!

A Glimpse Of Heaven

God created roses to
symbolize love
And give us a glimpse
of Heaven above.

God's Promise

It's just a humble rose dressed in
a cloak of red,
Yet it speaks of finer things and
summer days ahead.

Its beauty is a vision to uplift a
weary heart,
And in it God's created a priceless
work of art.

The garden now looks brighter,
And birds have come to sing,
I do believe my garden would
bring pleasure to a king!

When times seem dark and dreary
and you cannot carry on,
You may be uplifted by a poem or
a song,
Or a promise or a person or a
humble rose of red...
And that will be God's promise of
brighter days ahead!

In Case You've Forgotten

In Case you've forgotten, God uses...

The clouds in the sky
The butterfly
Summer showers
Beautiful flowers
The tree growing tall
The waterfall
The grass growing wild
The laugh of a child
A golden sunbeam
A flowing stream
The song from a bird
An encouraging word
The mighty seas
A gentle breeze

To remind us He is everywhere
And to let us know He's always near.

Living

'I want to see you live!'

Keep Living

When I die...
Please, don't die with me.
When I die...
Remember, you still have much to give.
When I die...
I'll watch over you from Heaven.
When I die...
I want to see you live!

A Spiritual Journey

Life is a spiritual journey from
the first day of our birth,
Life is a spiritual journey on this
beautiful planet called Earth.
Life is a spiritual journey -
we're here to learn all we can,
Life is a spiritual journey -
a special gift from God to man.

Living To Die

She is living to die
It makes you cry
To see life quietly pass her by.

She is living to die
I'm not sure why -
I've asked her but she won't reply.

She is living to die
Her life's a lie
She should be carving her name in the sky.

She is living to die
But still I'll try
To help her spread her wings...
And fly.

Knowing You

You would tell me to be brave
When I visit your grave.

You would tell me not to leave
flowers with the dead,
But to take them home and put
them in a vase instead.

You would tell me to embrace reality
Instead of a world I cannot see.

You would tell me to remember
your life as worthwhile,
And then you would tell me
to smile.

You would tell me I had
so much to give
And then you would tell me
to live!

Life Goes On

The day we depart
Somewhere
A new life will start.

Life goes on
When we have gone.

Love

'It was a privilege to have loved you!'

Miracles

Miracles happen every day,
They touch your life in the
strangest way
And they remind you that God,
in Heaven above,
Surrounds you each day with
His undying love.

The Many Years We Spent Together

The many years we spent together
were ones of love and caring,
Of fun and laughter, good and bad -
of togetherness and sharing.
They've filled my heart with memories,
so precious and so rare,
And I feel that I've been truly blest to
have shared them with you dear!

God's Love Is Everywhere

God's love is everywhere and in
every place you look,
You will find it in the pages of
the Holy Book,
You will find it in the garden, in
the flowers and the trees,
You will find it in tiny insects like
butterflies and bees.
You will find it in the springtime
and in the summer too,
It's true, God's love is everywhere
and in everything you do.
For God's love is infinite - it just
goes on and on...
You will hear it in children's laughter
and in the singing of a song.
It's in the oceans, in the forests
and in the valleys deep,
It's in the lovely dreams you have
when you are fast asleep.
But most of all and best of all you'll
find God's love, it's true,
Inside the heart of everyone - and
especially in you!

Privileged

It was a privilege to have loved you.
It was a privilege to know you loved
me too.
And when days have flown by and
others ask me what my fondest memory
of you is
I will simply tell them this -
It was a privilege to have loved you!

Love Is Immortal

Love is pure energy and
no matter how hard you try,
You can never kill love
because pure energy can't die.

The feeling of love can fade,
And the body can cease to give,
But the energy created by love
is immortal and continues
to live.

Preparing For Death

*'I welcome death with loving arms -
it holds no fear for me!'*

Fearless And Ready To Go

Dear ones, there's something you
need to know:
Death has knocked upon my door -
and I am ready to go.

I have no strength left within me
to stay and fight,
And I have no desire to - now
I've seen the light.

For the light of death is brighter
than the light of day,
And death's sweet voice is calling
me - calling me away.

So dear ones, very soon I know
that you will weep,
As my body falls into an everlasting
sleep.

But read these words I've written
once again, and you will see,
I welcome death with loving arms -
it holds no fear for me!

When I Have Gone

Don't be sad when I have gone,
be brave, shed not a tear,
For I'll have gone to a better place
where pain and anguish disappear.

Where God is love and all around
there's beauty to behold,
There's roses in the garden and
the streets are paved with gold.

There's a rainbow shining in the sky
and a white dove flying above,
And everyone is peaceful and their
hearts are filled with love.

And friends and family who have
passed this way before,
Will welcome me with open arms,
when I reach Heaven's door.

So when the time has come for me
to say goodbye,
Please be brave and strong and I
ask you not to cry...

For God will send His angels to
guide me on my way,
And I will live in paradise, loving
every day!

Suitcase Not Required

I'm going on a journey to a
place called Paradise,
I've read about it and to me
it sounds extremely nice.
I've got a one way ticket,
I'll be flying Angel Air,
Apparently they travel on
a wing and a prayer!

No, I don't plan on returning,
I'm going there to stay...
But please don't be too sad
because it's not that far away.
And besides, I will be having fun,
for there's lots to see and do...
And although you can't see me
I'll be able to see you!

Yes I'm going on a journey
when my time on Earth's expired,
To a place called Paradise
where no suitcase is required!

Without Fuss

Bury me in a simple box,
Keep my funeral plain,
Don't waste your money on
exotic wood or you might
hear me complain!

Give me a pillow to rest my head,
Then remember what I said -
"Money is for the living,
so don't waste it on the dead!"

Peace

'Go to your place of peace - relax'

An Unfamiliar Fabulous Feeling

And as I slowly closed my eyes I felt all
sensations cease,
And then I felt something unfamiliar
but fabulous...
Peace!

Free At Last

No more winters
No more rain
No more sorrow
No more pain.
No more problems
troubling me
No more tears
or misery.
No more quarrels
No more fear
No more hurt
No more despair.
No more working
for my keep
No more nightmares
when I sleep.
No more death
No more dying
No more grieving
No more crying.

No more these things,
they're now my past,
Because (thank God)
I'm free at last!

A Place Of Peace

Everyone needs a place of peace
to while away their cares,
A place to be all by yourself -
free from all despairs.

This peaceful place could be
your home
Where you feel safe and sound,
Or it could be a garden bench
with beauty all around.

A quiet corner to relax - unwind
and be at peace,
To recollect your inner thoughts
and feel your worries cease.

So when you're feeling weary -
plagued with stress and strain,
Go to your place of peace -
relax...
You'll feel at one again!

This Beautiful Garden

I could stand here for hours
in this beautiful garden,
I could stand here for hours
and never grow tired.
I could stand here for hours
in this beautiful garden,
And as each second passed
I'd become more inspired.
I could stand here for hours
in this beautiful garden,
Watching flowers grow and
winged-creatures fly.
I could stand here for hours
in this beautiful garden,
I could stand here for hours
and let the world pass me by...

Peace In Simplicity

I find peace in the early morn,
I find peace watching birds on my lawn;
I find peace beside the sea,
I find peace in simplicity;
I find peace at the end of the day,
I find peace when I stop and pray.

Remembrance

'The things I will miss about you most
are the things I will never forget!'

Rainbow

Colourful - that's how you must
remember me!

A lovable crazy fool who embraced
life tightly and absorbed it all.

Colourful - that's how I want my
funeral to be,
With colourful dress (no black please)
and flowers that are vibrantly beautiful.

Colourful - that's how you must learn
to see,
For with black and white vision you'll
never see me:
In the hues of summer flowers,
In the sparkling blue sea,
In the breathtaking sunset,
That's where I'll be.

Colourful - that's how you must
remember me!

Because Of You

Because of you,
The world is a much nicer place.

Because of you,
I have faith in the human race.

Because of you,
I know what it means to love
unconditionally.

Because of you,
I know what it means to give
unselfishly.

Because of you,
I believe in magic and mystery
and worlds unseen.

Because of you,
There is joy - wherever you are
and have ever been.

And all because of you!

Gone... But Not Forgotten

Death is a time to fondly remember
the laughter we shared and the
good times we had,
To know that your memory is secure
in my heart and will give me a lift
when I'm feeling sad.
Death is a time to realize with pride
just how lucky I was to call you
my friend,
To know that we shared an
understanding - a special bond right
up to the end.
Death is a time for realizing that
time alone will heal my pain,
And death is a time for nurturing my
spirit with the knowledge that someday
we'll meet up again.

Blessed

Blessed are those who knew you
And those who called you friend;
You enriched each life that
entered yours -
Right to the very end.

To Dear Diana

I wrote this poem in the Condolence Book for Princess Diana in The Cathedral, Christchurch, New Zealand on September 4, 1997

You were such a special person,
way beyond compare,
May God bless your gentle heart
and keep you in His care.

In Loving Memory

The things I will miss about you most
are these...

Your laugh, your smile, your desire
to please.
The little things which mean so much -
Your hugs, your kisses, your tender touch.
The way you always seemed to know
When somebody was feeling low.
The way your loving, warm embrace
Would put a smile on a weary face.
I'll miss your kindness, I'll miss your care,
I'll miss the good times we used to share.

And every time I think of you it will be
without regret -
Because the things I will miss about you
most are the things I will never forget!

His Legacy

At an early age he started to
create beauty.
The kind of beauty that could
reach in and touch your heart.
The kind of beauty that could
open your eyes - and bring a
tear to them at the same time.

He had vision - he could see the
future - even his own, I think.
And that's why, at an early age,
he started to create beauty.

His was to be a passionate life,
a creative life,
a meaningful life...
And a short life.

At an early age he started to
create beauty.
And that beauty is his legacy to
the world.

Sorrow

'I'm still managing to smile - on the outside'

Human

Dear Friend,

I thought you might like to know
you are not the only one who
feels this way.
Because today, millions of people
around the world feel the same
as you.
This may, or may not, be of help,
But it's true.

I just thought you'd like to know.

I Weep

Feeling...

Badder than bad
Madder than mad
Sadder than sad

I weep.

Grief

I'm screaming inside but I think it's okay -
I've been feeling sad since you went away.
And angry - yes, I'm angry too;
I'm angry at what I'm going through.

I'm angry to the point of going out of my mind
At the knowledge you're gone and I'm left behind.

It feels so cruel and it doesn't seem fair
That when I need you, you won't be there.
That when I want you, you won't be around -
I've lost you forever to the cold hard ground.

Some people believe in Heaven where the streets
are paved with gold,
But all I see is you, covered in snow, out in the cold.
Out in the hail, the wind and the rain - a slave to
the elements - and it fills me with pain.

So I'm screaming inside but I think it's okay -
I've been feeling sad since you went away.
But please don't avoid me, please don't run and hide
Because I'm still managing to smile - on the outside.

Gone Forever - Or So It Seems

Gone forever - or so it seems,
Gone are my aspirations, my hopes
and dreams.
Gone, it seems, is my will to forgive,
Gone is my will to love and to live.

Gone are the smiles I used to impart,
Gone is my soul and gone is my heart.
They have all gone for now, but those
who are clever
Know nothing is ever gone - forever!

Half-Hearted

How can I live,
What am I to do,
Now a part of my heart
Is buried with you?

Final Farewell

The good die young, that's what they say,
And it seems that they are right today;
For never will I meet again
A boy as sweet as you have been.

The road was dark, it sealed your fate...
When you saw the car it was too late.

So I'll wipe the teardrops from my face
At this, your final resting place.
And I feel for sure this is the end
As they bury my best friend.

About The Author

Faye Kilday was born in Christchurch, New Zealand in 1973. She wrote her first poem when she was five years old. She had her first poem published when she was sixteen.

Her first book of poems, *With Love xxx*, was published in 1996. She started writing Angel-Inspired Poetry in 1998 during an illness, when she had an angel experience. Her first book of Angel-Inspired Poetry, *Angels Speaking*, was published in 2000.

Her Angel-Inspired Poetry has been published on a variety of products including *Angel Guidance Cards*, Poetry Letters and Wallet Cards. Her poems have been published in national and international magazines. Faye also enjoys writing children's poetry.

For information on new books by Faye or to read more of her poems, please visit: **www.angel-inspiredpoetry.com**

Printed in the United Kingdom
by Lightning Source UK Ltd.
118337UK00001B/184-195

9 781847 284556